First Facts™

Community Helpers at Work

A Day in the Life of a
Librarian

by Judy Monroe

Consultant:
Hilary Sternberg
Head of Reference Services, E. H. Butler Library
Buffalo State College, State University of New York

Capstone
press

Mankato, Minnesota

First Facts is published by Capstone Press
151 Good Counsel Drive, P.O. Box 669, Mankato, Minnesota 56002
www.capstonepress.com

Library of Congress Cataloging-in-Publication Data
Monroe, Judy.
  A day in the life of a librarian / by Judy Monroe.
  p. cm.—(First facts. Community helpers at work)
  Includes bibliographical references and index.
  Contents: How do librarians start their days?—Who helps librarians?—Why do people use
the library?—What skills do librarians need?—How do librarians find everything?—Where do
library books come from?—How do librarians help the community?—How do librarians end
their days?
  ISBN 0-7368-2630-0 (hardcover)
  1. Librarians—Juvenile literature. 2. Libraries—Juvenile literature. [1. Librarians.
2. Occupations.] I. Title. II. Series.
Z682.M65 2005
020′.92—dc22   2003024652

Editorial Credits
Amanda Doering, editor; Jennifer Bergstrom, series designer; Molly Nei, book designer;
  Eric Kudalis, product planning editor

Photo Credits
All photographs by Capstone Press/Gary Sundermeyer, except page 20, Getty Images/Hulton
  Archive

Artistic Effects
Capstone Press/Gary Sundermeyer; PhotoDisc Inc.

Capstone Press thanks Kathie Kading and the Blue Earth County Library, Mankato, Minnesota,
  for their assistance in creating this book.

1 2 3 4 5 6 09 08 07 06 05 04

Table of Contents

How do librarians start their days?

Every day, librarians get the library ready for people to use. Kathie unpacks and checks in new books. She turns on the computers. She puts returned books on a cart. Kathie is ready to help people find information.

! Fun Fact!
About 137,000 librarians work in the United States.

Who helps librarians?

Assistants help librarians. They help people find and check out books. Assistants also put returned books back on the library shelves.

LIFE IN A BIOME

Life in an Ocean

Life in a Wetland

Life in a Desert

Life in a Forest

9:00 in the morning

Today, Kathie and her assistants make a **display**. They arrange books and objects on the same subject. This display teaches kids about life in different areas.

7

Why do people use the library?

People use the library to find many things. They can check out books, movies, and music to take home. Kathie helps a woman find a movie to watch.

8

Other people come to do **research**. They find information in books and magazines. Some people use the computers. Others study at the library.

10:30 in the morning

What skills do librarians need?

Librarians must like to help people. They teach people how to find information. Kathie helps a man find articles on the Internet.

12:00 in the afternoon

Librarians also need good computer skills. Kathie uses a **scanner** and computer to check out books. She uses a computer to keep track of library items.

11

How do librarians find everything?

All library items have call numbers. Call numbers tell people where to find items. Kathie helps a girl find books about cats. She types "cat" into the **computer catalog**. The call numbers of cat books come up on the screen. The call numbers match the numbers on books.

Fun Fact!
Librarians once listed everything in the library on small paper cards. The world's largest card catalog had about 60 million cards.

13

3:00 in the afternoon

14

Where do library books come from?

Librarians buy new items for the library. Kathie looks through catalogs to find new books, movies, and CDs. She also looks for damaged items on the shelves that need to be replaced.

How do librarians help the community?

Librarians plan programs for people in the **community**. Librarians plan story hours, book clubs, and summer reading programs. Today, Kathie reads to children at story hour.

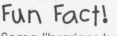

! Fun Fact!
Some librarians bring books to people in a bookmobile. A bookmobile is a van or truck with books that people can check out.

4:00 in the afternoon

17

How do librarians end their days?

Before she goes home, Kathie cleans her desk. She puts away papers. She checks her e-mail and then turns off her computer. Today, Kathie helped many people find books and information.

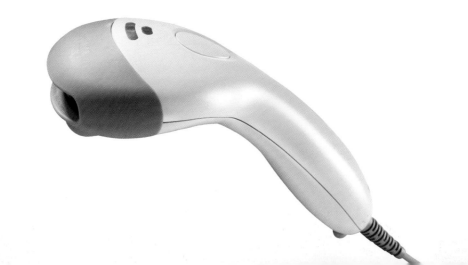

5:00 in the
afternoon

19

Amazing but True!

Until the late 1800s, children were not allowed in public libraries. The first children's room in a public library opened in 1895 in Boston, Massachusetts.

Computer

Scanner
Scanners read bar codes on books and library cards.

Book cart

Shelf

Book drop

21

Glossary

assistant (uh-SISS-tuhnt)—a person who helps someone else do a job

community (kuh-MYOO-nuh-tee)—a group of people who live in the same area

computer catalog (kuhm-PYOO-tur KAT-uh-log)—a list of all the items in a library; people can search on the computer catalog to find the items they want.

display (diss-PLAY)—a group of things organized to draw attention

research (REE-surch)—to study and learn about a subject

scanner (SKAN-uhr)—a machine that moves a beam of light over a code and sends the code information to a computer

Read More

Gorman, Jacqueline Laks. *Librarian.* People in My Community. Milwaukee: Weekly Reader Early Learning Library, 2002.

Miller, Heather. *Librarian.* This is What I Want to Be. Chicago: Heinemann, 2003.

Internet Sites

FactHound offers a safe, fun way to find Internet sites related to this book. All of the sites on FactHound have been researched by our staff.

Here's how:
1. Visit *www.facthound.com*
2. Type in this special code **0736826300** for age-appropriate sites. Or enter a search word related to this book for a more general search.
3. Click on the **Fetch It** button.

FactHound will fetch the best sites for you!

Index